Mittens are the motif of the month when it's cold outside. January is the perfect time to make this pillow or serve up some hot cocoa on a Mittens Mug Rug.

patterns on pages 18-19

Mittens Pillow and Mug Rug

'Be Mine' Mug Rug
Heartfelt Wall Hanging

Be My Valentine! Replace winter's cold with the heat of a passionate Valentine's Day. Bedeck your home with this bright red heartfelt wall hanging or cozy mug rug.

Use this pattern to spread the love to every room of the house. Turn the wall hanging into pillows in the living room, and decorate the dining table with a runner.

The Be Mine mug rug is perfect in the kitchen! Let your imagination run wild and have a heartfelt holiday.

patterns on pages 20-21

Luck 'O the Irish

St. Patrick's Day is an enchanted time - a day to begin transforming winter's dreams into summer's magic. ~Attributed to Adrienne Cook

These two charming projects will help you begin transforming your winter decor and bring a bit of the Luck o' the Irish into your home. You can have the greenest house on the block for St. Paddy's Day when you make these simple greetings. The wall hanging will also make a lovely pillow, and the punch needle can be applied to a shirt or purse...and that's no Blarney!

patterns on pages 22-23

Posey Flower Purse and Table Runner

Posey flowers start to bloom in your favorite room or anywhere you go with this handy purse.

Give Mom one of these beautiful projects for Mother's Day and she will have flowers all year long.

patterns on pages 24-25

Here comes Mister Cottontail!

Hop out to your favorite spring activity sporting this purse which features a punch needle bunny and all your friends will be asking where you bought that wonderful purse.

It will be so much fun to say, "I made it myself."

Announce your celebration of the arrival of Spring and welcome your guests with an Easter bunny wall hanging.

This fluffy bunny complements all your favorite holiday decorations, especially the colored eggs, bonnets and baskets of flowers.

patterns on pages 26-27

Cottontail Bunny Wall Hanging and Purse

Birds, Bees & Sunflowers

Frame a pretty set of punch needle birdhouses and celebrate your love of those feathered friends. If you plant some sunflowers in your garden, you will invite both birds and bees to visit.

Sensational sunflowers pair up with a busy beehive on a pillow that will bring cheer to your decor.

patterns on pages 28-30

Nostalgic Cape Cod

Make any room feel like a Cape Cod getaway with this nostalgic ensemble celebrating our country's heritage.

You can easily apply these colorful designs to a blanket, pillow, wall hanging, purse or sweatshirt.

patterns on page 32

What's Up Doc?

Bugs Bunny was never without a carrot. This carrot cloth adds a bit of whimsy to any table. Apply this simple carrots design to a place mat or hot pad for a complete ensemble or gift for the vegetarian in your family.

Or if you desire the serenity of a simple design in natural colors, you will want to make the Punch Needle carrots in the sage frame.

patterns on pages 34-35

May Flowers Purse

Make a purse in soft, sage fabric and decorate it with the natural tones of this May Flower punch needle design.

patterns on page 31

Luscious Fruit

Do you love a pear?

Do you love an apple?

Create these tempting framed Punch Needle fruits.

patterns on page 33

Say It with Flowers

Long celebrated as the flower of thoughts and remembrance, Pansies are one of nature's most delicate creations. Punch Needle art allows you to paint dimensional fiber flowers whose color never fades. This framed garden will last all year.

patterns on page 50

Autumn Leaves

Every Autumn, the earth graces us with a gorgeous array of falling leaves.

Recall the delight of jumping into that wonderful pile of color and crunch while you work on these leafy pieces of art.

Now you can express Autumn's natural colors in wool and fiber and use a lovely leaf motif to decorate your home or office.

patterns on pages 38-39

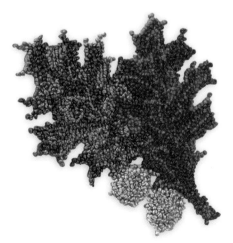

The Great Pumpkin

It's the Great Pumpkin!
Capture the excitement of the pumpkin patch and celebrate the earth's bounty with a pretty pumpkin table runner or framed Punch Needle embroidery.

patterns on pages 36-38

Believe...in Santa Pillow and Mug Rug

You are never too old to believe in Santa! Show off your holiday spirit with these seasonal Santa projects.

Even if you start in December, you will be able to finish these quick projects in time to enjoy the holiday season.

patterns on pages 40-42

"The stockings were hung by the chimney with care, in hopes that St. Nicholas soon would be there."

There's no better way to get into the holiday spirit than by making lovely decorations for your home and to give as gifts. These stocking projects will delight everyone on your list.

Make sure you check it twice so Santa has plenty to go around.

patterns on pages 43-46

Delightful Stockings

Christmas Treasures

Remember the joys of making Christmas cookies with Mama and Grandma?

Flour covered the counter and the whole house smelled of ginger, clove and vanilla.

Remember the first time you were allowed to measure the sugar? These gingerbread man projects will take you back to those wonderful days.

If you prefer snowmen or holly, these Punch Needle mug rugs are quick enough to make while you wait for the cookies to bake!

These pretty projects will make 'Thank You' gifts for the hostess at a holiday party, so make an extra!

patterns on pages 42, 46-49

Basic Directions for Punch Needle Embroidery

Materials:
Large 3-6 strand Punch Needle with threader
#5 Pearl Cotton or embroidery floss
6" locking type hoop
Small sharp scissors

Preparing a Punch Needle Project:

We recommend using Weaver's cloth for Punch Needle projects. It can be purchased at most fabric stores. Your fabric should be cut about 3" larger than the final project will be.

Punch needle is worked from the back, so the **design is printed in reverse**. Using tracing paper, trace the pattern and then transfer the Punch Needle design to the Weaver's cloth using a light table. Place the pattern on the light table. Center the Weaver's cloth over the pattern, and trace the pattern onto the Weaver's cloth using a sharp pencil.

Position Weaver's cloth in a hoop. Follow the manufacturer's instructions for using your needle tool.

You will need to refer to the color photos of each project to determine where each color is used.

Threading the Needle:

We use #5 Pearl Cotton so we used the largest tip of the Punch Needle. The needle size will vary on different brands.

There are 4 steps to threading the needle.

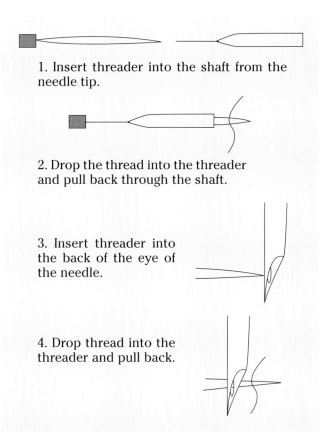

1. Insert threader into the shaft from the needle tip.

2. Drop the thread into the threader and pull back through the shaft.

3. Insert threader into the back of the eye of the needle.

4. Drop thread into the threader and pull back.

Setting the Depth:

All of our designs are punched at the lowest setting. Each brand of punch needle is different. Check your manual before beginning.

Punching:

Unroll the Pearl Cotton or untwine the floss before you thread the needle. Practice a straight row on a scrap of fabric. Keep the fabric pulled very tight in the hoop, in all directions, or your project may get distorted. Hold the hoop at an angle. Punch quickly, all the way down, pull up the tip of the needle just above the fabric.

You may hear a click when the needle brushes past the fabric. Move over and punch down again. The loops should be consistent, all the same size across. Don't punch too tightly. You should leave a space the thickness of the thread you are using. If not, try again. You'll quickly develop a rhythm.

Keep the open end of the needle (front) aimed towards the direction you are punching. The tail of the thread should follow you.

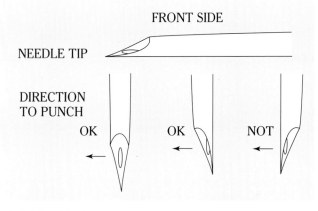

Finishing Projects

You have many choices to finish your punch needle projects.

1. You can fill in the background completely. Trim the edges within ½", fold under, and Whip Stitch to the back. You can mount it on a matboard to be framed or you can use a piece of wool for the background for framing.

2. You can punch only the design, leaving the Weaver's cloth showing on the background.

Press fabric flat after removing it from the hoop. You can use the Weaver's cloth as the background for your design when framing.

Size for Punch Needle

Basic Instructions for
Wool Work

**TIP: Wool can be done
with or without Fusible Web**

With Fusible Web:

1. Trace the pattern pieces onto the fusible web paper and roughly cut apart each piece.

2. Peel paper backing off of the fusible web and **press to the back of the wool** for 4-6 seconds.

3. Cut out each piece.

4. Peel the remaining paper backing off and position each piece on the wool background.

5. Place the pieces on the background fabric or wool in order.

6. Press to permanently bond for a minimum of 12 to 15 seconds. This will not permanently attach the wool but will hold it until hand stitching can be done.

7. Cool and pin for added hold.

8. Whipstitch or Buttonhole Stitch around each wool piece using Pearl Cotton #8 or thread.

9. Frame or make into a pillow or table runner.

Without Fusible Web:

1. Trace each pattern piece onto a plastic template and cut out. Use the templates to trace the wool pieces and cut each piece out.

2. Position and pin onto the backing fabric.

3. Whipstitch or Buttonhole stitch around each wool piece using Pearl Cotton #8 or thread.

Buttonhole or Blanket Stitch -

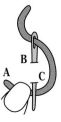

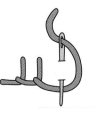

Come up at A, hold the thread down with your thumb, go down at B. Come back up at C with the needle tip over the thread. Pull the stitch into place. Repeat, outlining with the bottom legs of the stitch. Use this stitch to edge fabrics.

Mittens Mug Rug
Punch Needle - see page 17

SIZE: 3" x 4"

MATERIALS:
Weeks Dye Works #5 pearl cotton:
    Merlin #1305
    Pebble #1151 for background
    Amber #1224
    Snowflake #4125
    Angel Hair #1109
8" square Weaver's cloth
4¼" square of felt or wool to finish the back

INSTRUCTIONS:
1. Punch snowflakes on mittens using Snowflake.
2. Punch the trim on each mitten using Amber and Merlin.
3. Outline and fill in each mitten.
4. Outline and fill in background.
5. Make 2 rows around border using Snowflake.
6. Ties strings of Angel Hair pearl cotton on the mittens.
7. See page 17 for finishing instructions.

Mittens Pillow
Wool Work - see page 18

SIZE: 12" x 15"

MATERIALS:
Weeks Dye Works Wool:
    Two 12" x 15" Deep Sea #2104 for background
    Whiskey #2219 HB for mitten
    Whiskey #2219 HT for mitten
    Dungarees #2105 for Blue trim
DMC #5 pearl cotton (Cream #746, Blue #930)
Navy thread
Poly-Fil stuffing

PILLOW INSTRUCTIONS:

1. Cut 2 Deep Sea wool 12" x 15" for pillow.
2. Cut out 1 mitten from each color of Whiskey.
3. Cut out 2 of each trim piece from Dungarees wool.
4. Pin the mitten trim pieces to each mitten and Whipstitch using Navy thread.
5. Pin mitten to 1 of the 12" x 15" pieces of wool.
6. Buttonhole stitch outer edges of mittens using Blue pearl cotton.
7. Make snowflakes on mittens using Cream pearl cotton.
8. Stitch White tie lines across top of each mitten.
9. Tie a bow on top of 1 of the mittens.
10. Lay the 12" x 15" Blue rectangles right sides together.
11. Stitch around edges using a ¼" seam, leaving a 6" opening for turning.
12. Turn right side out. Push out corners.
13. Stuff firmly with Poly-Fil. Hand stitch opening closed.

Mittens
photo on page 3

Flap Purse A (rounded edge) & B (square edge)

B   A

A   B

Flap

HINT FOR MAKING WOOL PURSES:
You can make your purse doubled or from a single piece of wool. A doubled purse will have more stability, though a single purse will be lighter to carry. To make a doubled purse, cut 2 layers and stitch them together as a single layer.

Flap

side view

IMPORTANT:
Cut out an additional 7" long piece of paper and tape to bottom edge of template AB where indicated. This will give you a complete purse pattern piece.

BE MINE

Size for Punch Needle

Tape a 7" long piece of paper here.

Fold Line Add 7" to length

Heartfelt Hanging

Wool Work - see page 18

SIZE: 12½" x 12½""

MATERIALS:
Weeks Dye Works Wool:
      11" x 11" Louisiana Hot Sauce #2266 HT
        for inner background
      12½" x 12½" Red Pear #1332 HB for outer background
      Parchment #1110 for lace
      Red Pear #1332 HT for heart
DMC #5 pearl cotton Red #666 for letters
Thread (Tan, Pink, Red)

INSTRUCTIONS:
1. Cut out all of the pieces.
2. Freehand print the words "BE MINE" on the heart and stitch the words using Red pearl cotton #666.
3. Pin the lace edging on the center background square.
Buttonhole or Whip Stitch around lace edging to affix it to the background.
4. Attach the heart center using a Buttonhole stitch and Pink thread.
5. Attach the inner background to the outer background using a Buttonhole stitch and Red pearl cotton #666.

Be Mine Mug Rug

Punch Needle - see page 17

SIZE: 3½" x 3½"

MATERIALS:
Weeks Dye Works #5 pearl cotton:
      2 Camellia #2276
      Whitewash #1091
      2 Beige #1106
DMC #5 pearl cotton White
8" square Weaver's cloth
3½" square of felt or wool to finish the
      back

INSTRUCTIONS:
1. Punch the words "BE MINE" using White.
2. Punch lace edge around heart using Whitewash.
3. Fill in heart using Camellia.
4. Outline and fill in background with Beige.
5. See page 17 for finishing instructions.

Luck 'O the Irish

photo on page 5

Luck 'O
the Irish

Luck 'O the Irish
Wall Hanging
Wool Work - see page 18

SIZE: 11" x 12"

MATERIALS:
Weeks Dye Works wool:
    11" x 12" Collards #1277 for outer background,
    9" x 10" Parchment #1110 for inner background,
    Collards #1277 for the Shamrock
DMC #5 pearl cotton #895 for the Green letters

INSTRUCTIONS:
1. Cut out the shamrock from Collards wool.
2. Freehand print the words "Luck 'O The Irish" on the Parchment wool as shown.
3. Hand stitch words using *DMC* Green pearl cotton #895.
4. Pin the shamrock on the Parchment wool.
5. Buttonhole stitch around edges of shamrock using pearl cotton #895.
6. Center the Parchment wool on the Collards wool outer background.
7. Buttonhole stitch around edges of Parchment wool using pearl cotton #895.
8. Finish: Sew 2 tabs on the top back of the wall hanging and insert a stick if desired.

Luck 'O the Irish
Punch Needle - see page 17

SIZE: 3" x 4"

MATERIALS:
Weeks Dye Works #5 pearl cotton:
    2 Beige #1106
    Emerald #2171
DMC #5 pearl cotton Green #367 for letters
8" square Weaver's cloth
4½" square of felt or wool to finish the back or
5" x 7" frame

INSTRUCTIONS:
1. Punch the words "Luck 'O the Irish" using *DMC* #367 pearl cotton.
2. Punch the shamrock using the hand-dyed Emerald.
3. Outline and fill in background using Beige.
4. See page 17 for finishing instructions.

Size for Punch Needle

Posey Flower Table Runner and Purse

photo on page 6

Posey Flower Purse

Wool Work - see page 18

SIZE: Purse 7" x 7½", Strap 24"

MATERIALS:
Purse template A on page 20
Weeks Dye Works Wool:
      7" x 18" Gunmetal #1298 for Purse
      Lancaster #1333 for Flower
      Kudzu #2200 for Leaves
DMC #5 pearl cotton (Pink #221, Green #3052)
1" Dark Red button
25" Cording or drapery tie-back for purse strap

INSTRUCTIONS:
1. Cut 1 purse using template A from Gunmetal wool.
2. Using the patterns from the Flower Table Runner:
      Cut out 1 flower from Lancaster Red wool.
      Cut out 3 leaves from Kudzu Green wool.
3. Position leaves and flower on lower front of purse.
4. Buttonhole stitch leaves and flowers to the purse using matching pearl cotton.

5. Make French knots in center of flower using Green pearl cotton.
6. Fold purse at fold line.
7. Using *DMC* #3052: Buttonhole stitch up 1 side of purse through both layers, across flap through a single layer, and down the other side through both layers.
8. Sew button on purse under the flap.
9. Cut a slit for the buttonhole in the purse flap and Buttonhole stitch around the slit.
10. Using cording or a drapery tie-back for strap, hand stitch the ends to either side of the upper edge of purse under the flap.

> **HINT FOR MAKING WOOL PURSES:**
> You can make your purse doubled or from a single piece of wool. A doubled purse will have more stability, though a single purse will be lighter to carry. To make a doubled purse, cut 2 layers and stitch them together as a single layer.

Posey Flower Table Runner

Wool Work - see page 18

SIZE: 16" x 23"

MATERIALS:
Use Table Runner Corner templates A & B on page 38.
Weeks Dye Works Wool:
      Parchment #1110 for inner background
      Kudzu #2200 for outer background
      Lancaster Red #1333 for flowers
      Meadow #2176 HB for leaves
DMC #8 pearl cotton:
      Rust #355 around flowers
      Emerald Green #3345 around leaves
      Gold #783 for French knots

INSTRUCTIONS:
1. From Parchment wool, cut out 15" x 22" rectangle.
2. Using template A, round corners of Parchment color wool piece.
3. From Kudzu wool, cut out 16" x 23" rectangle.
4. Using template B, round corners of Kudzu wool piece.
5. The flowers and leaves are numbered and lettered for your tracing convenience.
6. Using Lancaster Red wool, cut out 6 flowers, 2 of each number.
7. From Meadow wool, cut out 8 leaves, 2 of each letter.
8. Position & pin flowers and leaves on Parchment wool top.
9. Using Buttonhole stitch, attach flowers and leaves to top.
10. With Gold pearl cotton, make French knots in the center of the flowers.
11. Lay Parchment wool top on top of Green wool piece.
12. Buttonhole stitch around the outer edge to attach the two wools together.

Placement for Table Runner

A

B

C

2

D

1

3

Bunny

photo on page 6-7

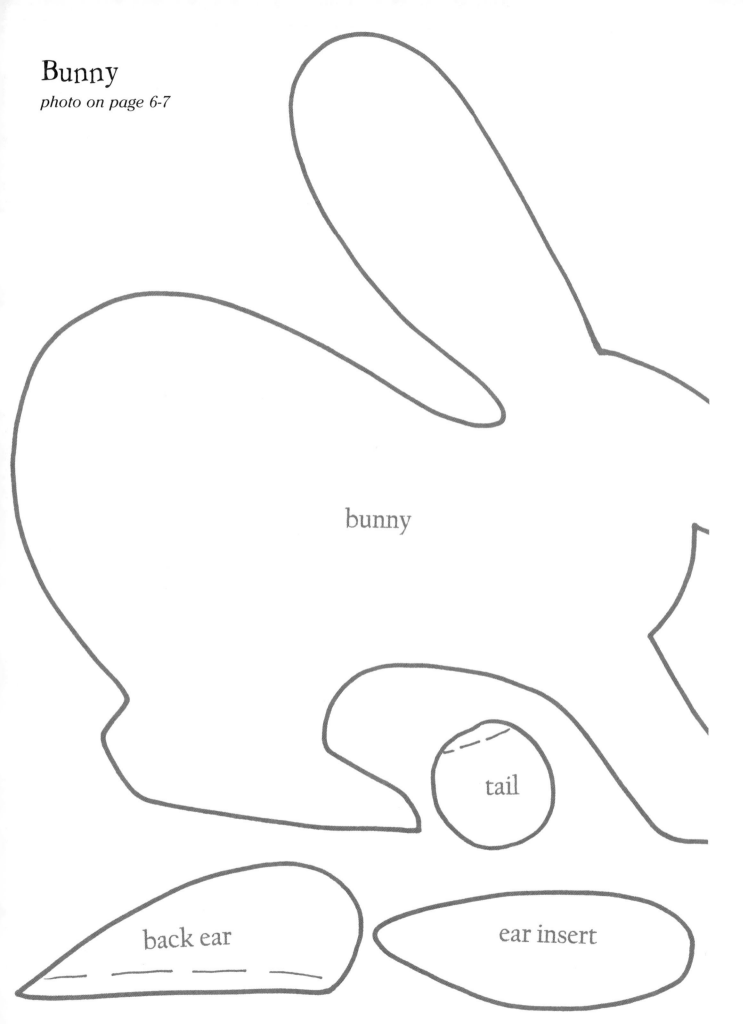

bunny

tail

back ear

ear insert

Bunny Purse

Punch Needle - see page 17

SIZE: Purse 7" x 7¼", Strap 23"
Punch needle patch 3½" x 4"

MATERIALS:

Purse:
Use template A on page 20
Weeks Dye Works Red Pear #1332 HT wool
⅞" Deep Pink button
DMC #5 pearl cotton Green #502
24" Cream cording or drapery tie-back for strap

Punch needle:
Weeks Dye Works #5 pearl cotton:
    2 Sea Foam #1166 for background
    2 Fawn #1111 for bunny
    Hibiscus #2278 for nose and ears
    Charcoal #1303 for eye
8" Weaver's Cloth

INSTRUCTIONS:
1. Punch center of front ear and nose in Hibiscus, the eye in Charcoal, the bunny in Fawn, and the background in Sea Foam.
2. Trim the Weaver's cloth to within ½" of punch needle.
3. Fold the edges under and Whipstitch to the back of the punch needle project.
4. From template A, cut 1 purse from Red Pear HT wool.
5. Fold purse on fold line.
6. Buttonhole stitch up 1 side of the purse through both layers, around the flap through a single layer, and down other side of purse again through both layers using pearl cotton #502.
7. Whipstitch punch needle to front of purse.
8. Sew button to the purse under the flap.
9. Cut a slit in the flap for the buttonhole and Buttonhole stitch around the slit.
10. Use cording or a drapery tie-back for the strap. Hand stitch the ends to either side of the upper edge of the purse under the flap.

> **HINT FOR MAKING WOOL PURSES:**
> You can make your purse doubled or from a single piece of wool. A doubled purse will have more stability, though a single purse will be lighter to carry. To make a doubled purse, cut 2 layers and stitch them together as a single layer.

Size for Punch Needle

Bunny Wall Hanging

Wool Work - see page 18

SIZE: 12" x 15"

MATERIALS:
Weeks Dye Works Wool:
    10" x 13" Hand-dyed Green for inner background
    12" x 15" Parchment #1110 for outer background
    Parchment #1110 for bunny body
    Sand #3500 for rear ear
    Red Pear #1332 for inner ear
    Raw wool for tail
DMC #5 pearl cotton :
    Charcoal #3021 for French knot eye
    Pink #760 for nose
    Color to match the Green wool background
Tan thread

INSTRUCTIONS:
1. Cut out all pieces and assemble them on the Green wool background piece.
2. Using Tan color thread, Buttonhole stitch or Whipstitch around each piece to affix it to the Green wool.
3. Use Charcoal pearl cotton to make a French knot for the eye.
4. Use Pink pearl cotton to make the nose.
5. Make bunny tail using raw wool.
6. Roll raw wool into a ball and tack to rear end of bunny with a hand stitch.
7. Center the Green color wool on top of the Parchment wool background piece.
8. Buttonhole stitch around the edges of the Green wool piece to affix it to the Parchment wool background.

Birdhouses & Beehives

photo on page 8

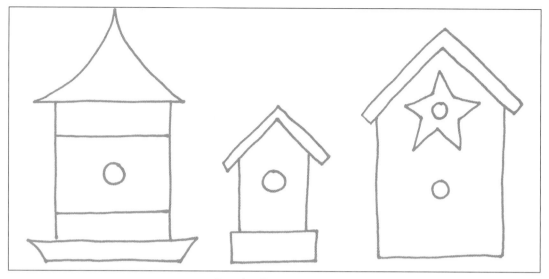

Size for Punch Needle

Framed Birdhouse

Punch Needle - see page 17

SIZE: Punch needle patch 2¾" x 5¾"

MATERIALS:

Weeks Dye Works #5 pearl cotton:
    2 Fawn #1111 for background
    Dolphin #1296
    Twilight #1285
    Whiskey #2219

8" x 9" Weavers cloth
5 x 7" frame

INSTRUCTIONS:
1. Punch birdhouse holes using Twilight.
2. Punch Whiskey sections on birdhouses.
3. Punch Dolphin sections on birdhouses.
4. Punch Twilight sections on birdhouses.
5. Punch outline and fill in background with Fawn.
6. See page 17 for finishing instructions.

Beehive Mug Rug

Punch Needle - see page 17

SIZE: 3¾" x 4"

MATERIALS:

Weeks Dye Works #5 pearl cotton:
    2 Charcoal #1303
    Gold #2221
    Scuppermong #2196
    Light Khaki #1101
DMC #5 pearl cotton Brown #433
8" square Weaver's cloth
3½" x 4" felt or wool for finishing the back

INSTRUCTIONS:
1. Punch the hole & the single lines of Brown on beehive.
2. Outline and fill in remainder of beehive using Gold.
3. Punch center of flowers using Brown #433.
4. Punch flowers using Light Khaki.
5. Punch leaves using Scuppermong.
6. Outline and fill in background using Charcoal.
7. See page 17 for finishing instructions.

Size for Punch Needle

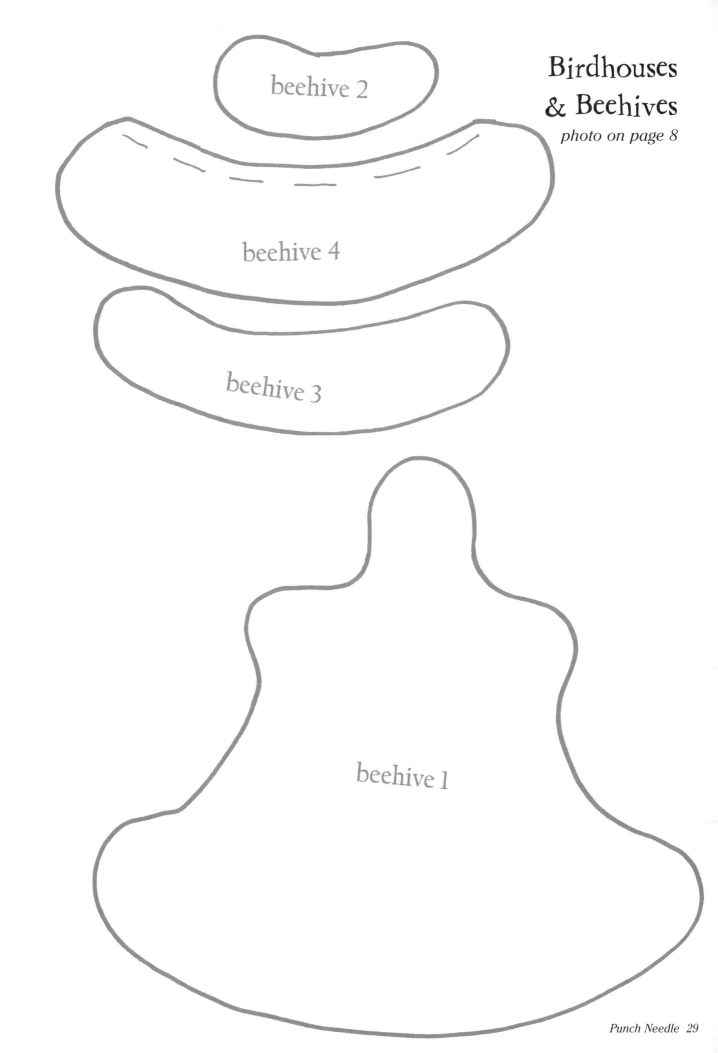

beehive 2

beehive 4

beehive 3

beehive 1

Birdhouses & Beehives

photo on page 8

Placement for Pillow

Beehive Pillow

Wool Work - see page 18

SIZE: 13" x 14"

MATERIALS:

Weeks Dye Works Wool:
    Two 13" x 14" Black
    Mustard #1224 for flowers
    Palomino #1232 for hive
    Mustard #1224 HB for hive
    Mustard #1224 HT for hive
    Chestnut #1269 for flower centers
    Collards #1277 for leaves
Brown thread
Poly-Fil stuffing

INSTRUCTIONS:

CUTTING:
    Two 13" x 14" pieces from Black wool.
    1 of pattern #1 from Palomino wool.
    1 each of patterns #2 and #4 from
Mustard HT wool.
    1 of pattern #3 from Mustard HB wool.
    2 leaves from Green wool.
    2 flowers from Mustard solid wool.
    2 flower centers from Chestnut wool.

ASSEMBLY:

1. On one of the 13" x 14" Black wool rectangles, position the pieces.
2. Whipstitch in place using Brown thread.
3. Lay the 13" x 14" Black rectangles with right sides together.
4. Stitch around the edges using a ¼" seam, leaving a 6" opening for turning.
5. Turn right side out. Push out corners.
6. Stuff firmly with Poly-Fil. Hand stitch opening closed.

A HELPFUL HINT ABOUT WOOL PILLOW ASSEMBLY:

To cut down on the amount of Poly-Fil used and to make your pillow "smoother", you may wish to cut out 2 pieces of cotton batting 1" larger (all the way around) than your pillow front and back pieces.

Lay the wool pillow back and front pieces right sides together and place the 2 batting pieces below them. In other words, you will have a "sandwich" consisting of 2 batting pieces on the bottom, the wool pillow front, and the wool pillow back. Stitch through all four layers.

After you turn the pillow right side out, stuff BETWEEN the 2 layers of batting.

May Flowers Purse
Punch Needle - see page 17

SIZE:
  Purse: 7" x 7¼", Strap 26"
  Punch needle patch 3¼" x 3¾"

MATERIALS:

Purse:
Use Purse Template A on page 20
Weeks Dye Works wool Kudzu #2200
Green ⅞" button
27" Gold cording or drapery tie-back for strap
DMC #5 pearl cotton Gold/Tan #422

Punch needle:
Weeks Dye Works #5 pearl cotton:
  2 Sage #1246 for background
  Blue Spruce #1276 for leaves
  Curry #2220 for flower centers
  Angel Hair #1109 for flowers
8" square Weaver's cloth

INSTRUCTIONS:
1. Punch the flower centers in Curry, the flowers in Angel hair, the leaves in Blue Spruce, and background in Sage.
2. Trim the Weaver's cloth to within ½" of punch needle.
3. Fold the edges under and Whipstitch to the back of the punch needle project.
4. From from Kudzu wool, cut out 1 purse using template A.
5. Fold purse on fold line. Using Gold/Tan pearl cotton: Buttonhole stitch up 1 side of the purse through both layers, around the flap through a single layer, and down the other side of purse through both layers.
6. Whipstitch punch needle to front of purse.
7. Sew a button to the purse under the flap.
8. Cut a slit in the flap for the buttonhole and Buttonhole stitch around the slit.
9. Use cording or a drapery tie-back for the strap. Hand stitch the ends to either side of the upper edge of the purse under the flap.

Size for Punch Needle

HINT FOR MAKING WOOL PURSES:
  You can make your purse doubled or from a single piece of wool. A doubled purse will have more stability, though a single purse will be lighter to carry. To make a doubled purse, cut 2 layers and stitch them together as a single layer.

Cape Cod Americana

photo on page 9

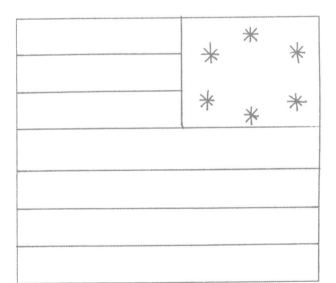

Boat

Punch Needle - see page 17

SIZE: Punch needle 3" x 3¼"

MATERIALS:
Weeks Dye Works #5 pearl cotton:
    Deep Sea #2104, Liberty #2269
DMC #5 pearl cotton (Gold #783, Cream #746)
8" x 9" Weavers cloth
4" x 6" frame

INSTRUCTIONS:
1. Punch Navy Blue sections of boat with Deep Sea.
2. Punch Gold boat sail.
3. Punch Red areas of boat with Liberty.
4. Punch background with Cream color.
5. See page 17 for finishing instructions.

1776 Flag

Punch Needle - see page 17

SIZE: Punch needle 3½" x 3¾"

MATERIALS:
Weeks Dye Works #5 pearl cotton:
    Merlin #1305, Garnet #2264, Angel Hair #1109
8" square Weavers cloth
8" x 10" frame

INSTRUCTIONS:
1. Punch stars on flag using Angel Hair.
2. Fill in Navy Blue areas with Merlin.
3. Punch the number "1776" with Merlin.
4. Punch Red sections of flag with Garnet.
5. Punch Cream color sections of flag with Angel Hair.
6. Fill in background if desired.
7. See page 17 for finishing instructions.

Flag Star Purse

Punch Needle
- see page 17

SIZE: Punch needle 3½" x 4", Purse 7" x 7¼", Strap 35"

MATERIALS:

For Purse:
Template B on page 20
Weeks Dye Works Dungarees #2105 wool for Purse
1 Dark Red 1" button
DMC #5 Cream #712 pearl cotton
36" Cream-colored cording or drapery tie-back for strap

For Punch Needle:
Weeks Dye Works #5 pearl cotton Navy #1306
DMC #5 (Red #816, Cream #712)
8" square Weaver's Cloth

INSTRUCTIONS:
1. To make the punch needle star: Punch the Navy Blue section first. Punch Cream color section next. Punch the Red section last.
2. Trim the Weaver's cloth to within ½" of punch needle design.
3. Fold under the excess Weaver's cloth and Whipstitch to the back of punch needle project.
4. From Dungarees wool, cut 1 purse using template B.
5. Fold purse in half at fold line. Using Cream color pearl cotton:
6. Buttonhole stitch up 1 side of purse through both layers. Continue across the flap stitching through 1 layer, and down the other side again through both layers .
7. Whipstitch the star to the front of the purse.
8. Sew a button under the flap.
9. Cut a slit in purse flap for a buttonhole and Buttonhole stitch around the slit.
10. Use cording or a drapery tie-back for the strap. Hand stitch the ends to either side of the upper edge of the purse under the flap.

> **HINT FOR MAKING WOOL PURSES:**
> You can make your purse doubled or from a single piece of wool. A doubled purse will have more stability, though a single purse will be lighter to carry. To make a doubled purse, cut 2 layers and stitch them together as a single layer.

Apple

Punch Needle
- see page 17

SIZE: Punch needle 3" x 4"
MATERIALS:
Weeks Dye Works #5 pearl cotton:
    2 Turkish Red #2266
    Ivy #2198
DMC #5 pearl cotton (Ecru, Brown #610)
8" square Weaver's cloth
5" x 7" oval frame

INSTRUCTIONS:
1. Punch stem with Brown.
2. Punch leaf with Ivy.
3. Outline and fill in apple with Turkish Red.
4. Fill in shadow below apple with Ecru.
5. This background was not filled in, but may be filled in if desired.
6. See page 17 for finishing instructions.

Pear

Punch Needle
- see page 17

SIZE:
Punch needle 3¼" x 4"

MATERIALS:
Weeks Dye Works #5 pearl cotton:
    Scuppermong #2196
    Ivy #2198
    Whitewash #1091
DMC (Ecru, Brown #610)
8" square Weaver's cloth
5" x 7" oval frame

INSTRUCTIONS:
1. Punch stem with Brown.
2. Punch leaf with Ivy.
3. Punch highlighted area on pear using Whitewash.
4. Outline and fill in pear with Scuppermong.
5. Punch shadow below pear with Ecru color.
6. See page 17 for finishing instructions.

Framed Fruit

photo on page 11

Carrot Table Mat and Framed Art

photo on page 10

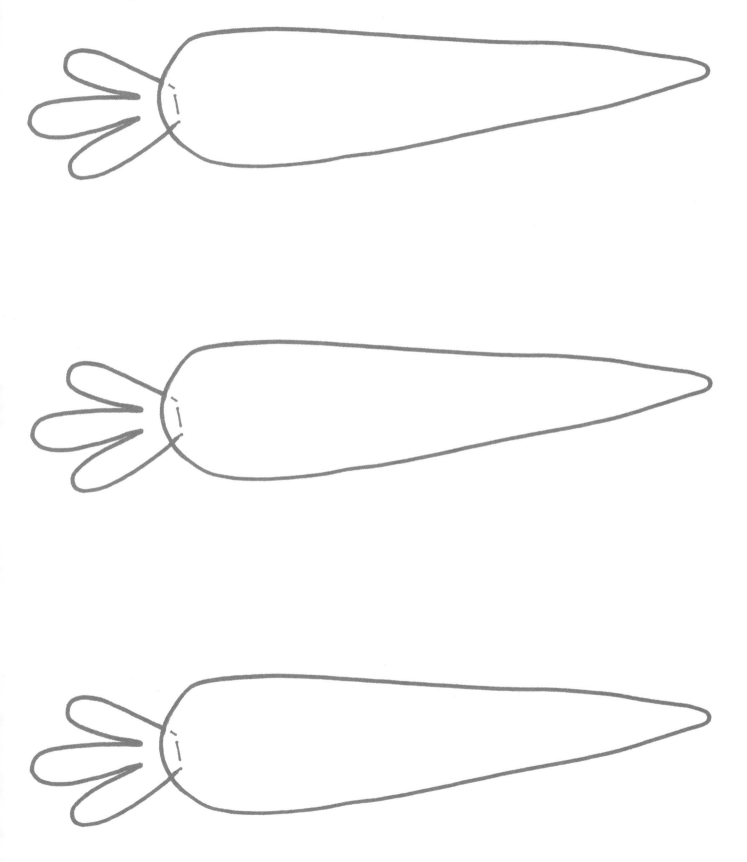

Carrot Table Mat and Framed Art

photo on page 10

Framed Carrots

Punch Needle - see page 17

SIZE: Punch needle 4" x 4"

MATERIALS:

Weeks Dye Works #5 pearl cotton:
>   2 Carrot #2226
>   2 Beige #1106 for background

DMC #5 pearl cotton (Green #3052 for carrot tops, Rust #301 for veins)

8" x 9" Weaver's cloth

5" x 7" frame

INSTRUCTIONS:

1. Punch the veins on the carrots.
2. Punch the carrot tops.
3. Punch carrot outline and fill in carrot center.
4. Punch background outline and fill in using swirling pattern.
5. Using Green pearl cotton, make 2 rows around border.
6. See page 17 for finishing instructions.

Size for Punch Needle

Carrot Table Mat

Wool Work - see page 18

SIZE: 15" x 23"

MATERIALS:

Weeks Dye Works Wool:
>   14" x 22" piece of Birch #1197 for inner background
>   15" x 23" piece of Sweet Potato #2238 HT for outer background
>   Carrot #2226 for carrots
>   Meadow #2176 for carrot tops

#5 pearl cotton to match each background

Tan thread

INSTRUCTIONS:

1. Cut 14" x 22" piece of Birch wool.
2. Cut 15" x 23" piece of Sweet Potato wool.
3. Cut out 6 carrots and 6 carrot tops.
4. Position 3 carrots and carrot tops on each end of Birch wool piece.
5. Using Tan thread, Buttonhole stitch around each carrot and carrot top to affix them to Birch wool piece.
6. Lay the Birch rectangle on top of the Sweet Potato rectangle.
7. Using matching pearl cotton, Buttonhole stitch around the outer edges of the Birch wool piece to attach it to the Sweet Potato wool piece.
8. Using matching pearl cotton, Buttonhole stitch around the outer edges of the Sweet Potato wool piece.

Pumpkins

photo on page 13

C

D

A

Pumpkin Table Runner
Wool Work - see page 18

SIZE: 15" x 30"

MATERIALS:
Template B on page 38
1 yard Black wool felt
Weeks Dye Works Wool:
>   Terra Cotta #2239 HT for pumpkins
>   Terra Cotta #2239 for pumpkin center
>   Juniper #2158 HB for leaves
>   Chestnut #1269 for stems

DMC #8 pearl cotton Black #310

INSTRUCTIONS:
1. Cut a 15" x 30" piece of Black wool felt.
2. Use the rounded edge of Template B on page 38 to round the edges into an oval shape.
3. From Terra Cotta HT, cut out 2 pumpkin A pieces.
4. From Terra Cotta solid, cut out 2 pumpkin B pieces.
5. Cut out 2 leaves C and 2 leaves D from Green wool.
6. Cut out 2 stems from Brown wool.
7. Position a stem on each end and then layer A, then B, then C, then D on each end.
8. Pin pieces in place.
9. Using Black pearl cotton, Buttonhole stitch around each piece.

photo on page 12

Framed Pumpkin

Punch Needle - see page 17

SIZE: Punch needle 3" x 3½"

MATERIALS:

Weeks Dye Works #5 pearl cotton:
   2 Pumpkin #2228
   Ivy #2198 for greenery
   Beige #1106 for background

DMC #5 pearl cotton Cocoa #839 for stem, lines and border

8" square Weaver's cloth

5" x 7" frame

INSTRUCTIONS:

1. Punch Brown on inner lines to separate pumpkin sections.
2. Punch stem using Brown pearl cotton.
3. Punch leaves using Green pearl cotton.
4. Punch outline and fill in pumpkin.
5. Punch outline and fill in background using Beige pearl cotton.
6. Using Cocoa pearl cotton, punch 2 rows for border.
7. See page 17 for finishing instructions.

Size for Punch Needle

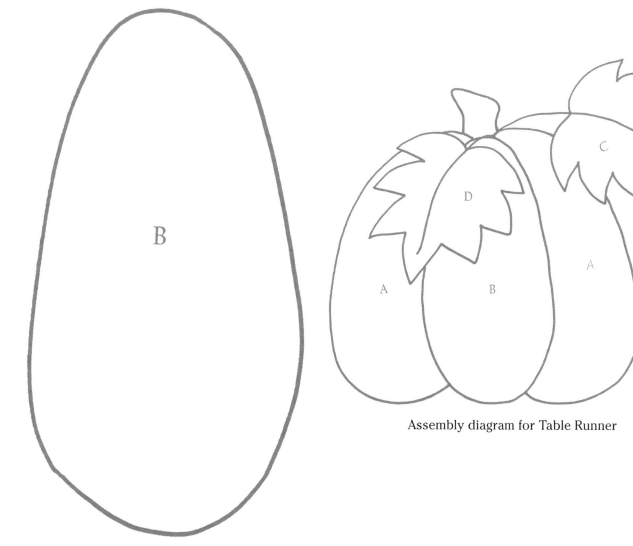

Assembly diagram for Table Runner

Autumn Leaves

photo on page 12

Outer edge

Table runner corner cutting guide

Inner edge

B

A

Center line

Table Runner

Size for Punch Needle

Framed Leaves

**Punch Needle
- see page 17**

SIZE:
Punch needle 4" x 4"

MATERIALS:
Weeks Dye Works #5 pearl cotton:
    2 Ivy #2198
    2 Terra Cotta #2239
    Conch #1133
8" square Weaver's cloth
5" x 7" frame

INSTRUCTIONS:
1. Punch acorn using Conch.
2. Punch Ivy leaf.
3. Punch Terra Cotta leaf.
4. See page 17 for finishing instructions.

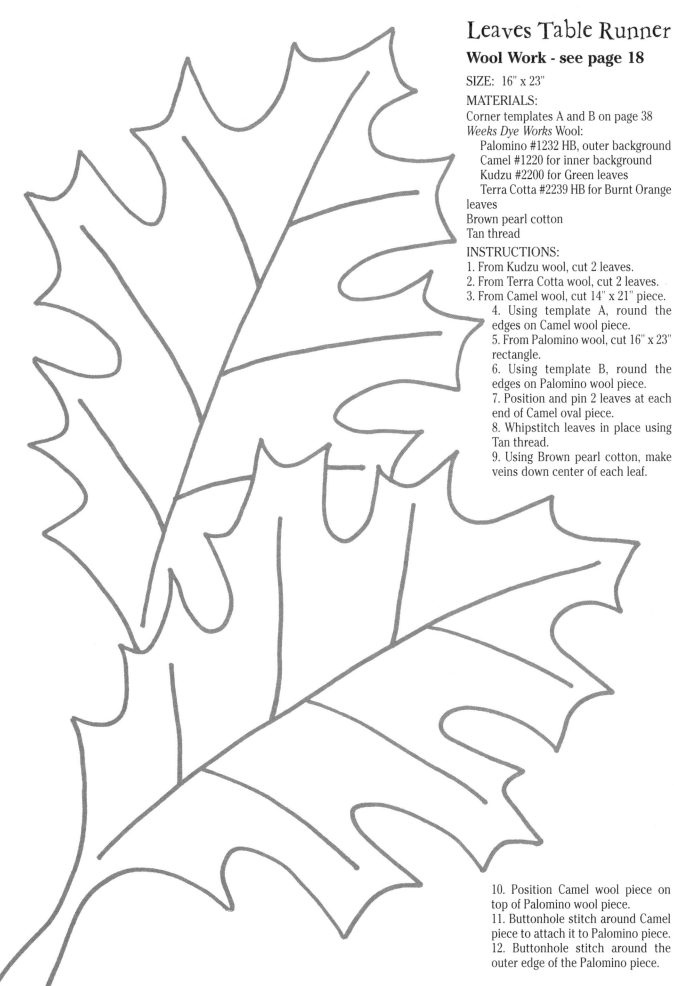

Leaves Table Runner
Wool Work - see page 18

SIZE: 16" x 23"

MATERIALS:

Corner templates A and B on page 38

Weeks Dye Works Wool:
Palomino #1232 HB, outer background
Camel #1220 for inner background
Kudzu #2200 for Green leaves
Terra Cotta #2239 HB for Burnt Orange leaves

Brown pearl cotton

Tan thread

INSTRUCTIONS:

1. From Kudzu wool, cut 2 leaves.
2. From Terra Cotta wool, cut 2 leaves.
3. From Camel wool, cut 14" x 21" piece.
4. Using template A, round the edges on Camel wool piece.
5. From Palomino wool, cut 16" x 23" rectangle.
6. Using template B, round the edges on Palomino wool piece.
7. Position and pin 2 leaves at each end of Camel oval piece.
8. Whipstitch leaves in place using Tan thread.
9. Using Brown pearl cotton, make veins down center of each leaf.

10. Position Camel wool piece on top of Palomino wool piece.
11. Buttonhole stitch around Camel piece to attach it to Palomino piece.
12. Buttonhole stitch around the outer edge of the Palomino piece.

Do You Believe?

photo on page 14

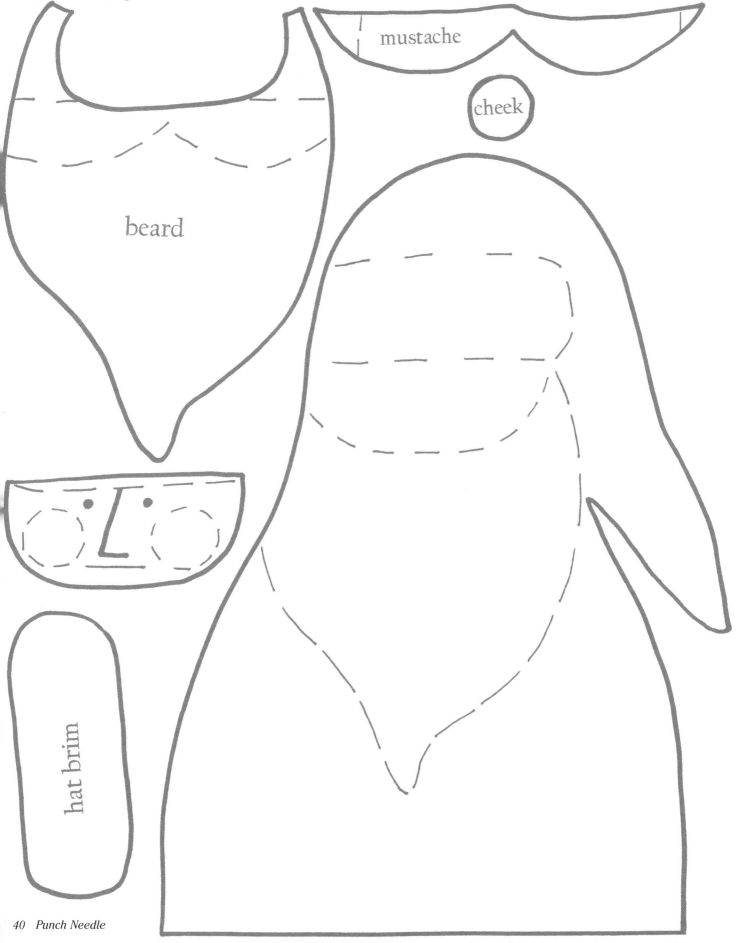

mustache

cheek

beard

hat brim

Believe Pillow

Wool Work - see page 18

SIZE: 11" x 14"

MATERIALS:

Weeks Dye Works Wool:
> Two 11" x 14" pieces of Merlot #1334 for pillow front and back
> One 10" x 13" piece of #3500 Sand HT for back ground
> Merlot #1334 HT for body
> Merlot #1334 for hat
> Parchment #1110 for hat brim and mustache
> Sand #3500 for beard
> Red Pear #1332 for cheeks

DMC #5 pearl cotton
> (Red #115, Black #310, Ecru for the tassel)

Tan thread

Poly-Fil stuffing

INSTRUCTIONS:

CUTTING:
> Two 11" x 14" pieces from Merlot wool.
> One 10" x 13" piece from Sand HT wool.
> Mustache and hat brim from Parchment wool.
> Beard and face from Sand wool.
> Cheeks from Red Pear wool.
> Hat from Merlot solid wool.
> Body from Merlot HT wool.

ASSEMBLY:

1. Using pencil, freehand print the word "Believe!" on top of 10" x 12" Sand HT wool rectangle.
2. Stitch the word using *DMC* Red pearl cotton.
3. Position body pieces on 10" x 13" Sand HT wool rectangle and Whipstitch using Tan thread.
4. Using Black pearl cotton, stitch nose and make 2 French knots for eyes.
5. Center Sand HT wool rectangle on top of Merlot wool rectangle.
6. Make a running stitch on Sand wool piece ¼" away from edge using Red pearl cotton to attach it to the Merlot colored wool rectangle.
7. Tie a tassel on the tip of Santa's hat using Ecru pearl cotton.
8. Lay the 2 Merlot wool rectangles right sides together.
9. Stitch around outer edges using a ¼" seam, leaving 6" opening for turning.
10. Turn right side out. Push out corners.
11. Stuff firmly with Poly-Fil.
12. Hand stitch opening closed.

Placement for Pillow

A HELPFUL HINT ABOUT WOOL PILLOW ASSEMBLY:

To cut down on the amount of Poly-Fil used and to make your pillow "smoother", you may wish to cut out 2 pieces of cotton batting 1" larger (all the way around) than your pillow front and back pieces.

Lay the wool pillow back and front pieces right sides together and place the 2 batting pieces below them. In other words, you will have a "sandwich" consisting of 2 batting pieces on the bottom, the wool pillow front, and the wool pillow back. Stitch through all four layers.

After you turn the pillow right side out, stuff BETWEEN the 2 layers of batting.

Do You Believe?

photo on page 14

Size for Punch Needle

Size for Punch Needle

Santa Mug Rug

Punch Needle - see page 17

SIZE: Punch needle 3¼" x 3½"

MATERIALS:
Weeks Dye Works #5 pearl cotton:
    Turkish Red #2266
    Light Khaki #1101 for beard
    2 Charcoal #1303 for background
DMC #5 pearl cotton:
    Ecru for mustache and hat
    Rose #758 for cheeks
    Flesh #951 for face
8" square Weaver's cloth
3½" square of felt or wool to finish the back

INSTRUCTIONS:
1. Punch cheeks & nose using Rose.
2. Punch face using Flesh.
3. Punch moustache using Ecru.
4. Punch beard using Light Khaki.
5. Punch hat brim and tip of hat with Ecru.
6. Punch hat and body using Turkish Red.
7. Outline and fill in background using Charcoal.
8. Using Charcoal, make 2 French knots for eyes.
9. See page 17 for finishing instructions.

Holly Mug Rug

Punch Needle - see page 17

SEE PHOTO ON PAGE 16

SIZE: 3½" x 3½"

MATERIALS:
Weeks Dye Works #5 pearl cotton:
    Holly #1279
    2 Light Khaki #1101
DMC #5 pearl cotton (Red #817, Black #310)
8" square Weaver's cloth
3½" square felt or wool to finish the back

INSTRUCTIONS:
1. Punch veins in leaves using Black.
2. Fill in leaves using Holly.
3. Punch the berries using Red.
4. Outline and fill in background using Light Khaki.
5. See page 17 for finishing instructions.

Stockings

photo on page 15

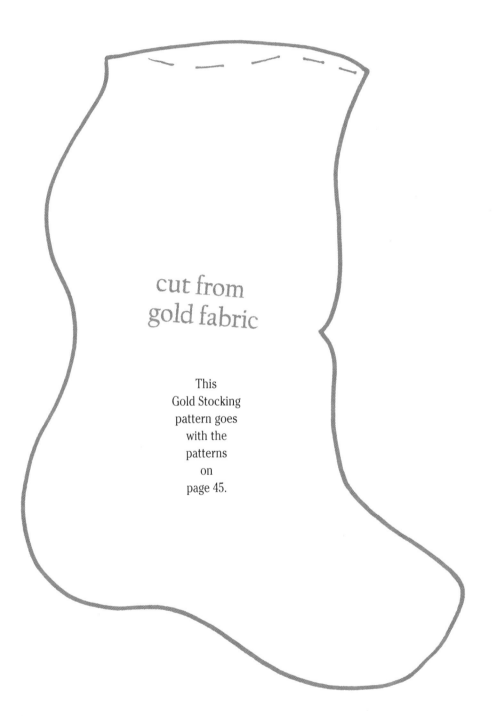

cut from
gold fabric

This
Gold Stocking
pattern goes
with the
patterns
on
page 45.

Stockings

photo on page 15

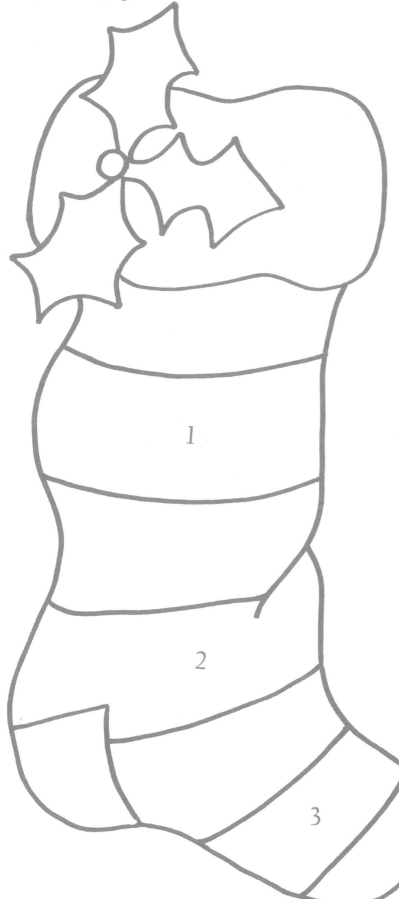

Stocking Wall Hanging
Wool Work - see page 18

SIZE: 13" x 15"

MATERIALS:

Weeks Dye Works Wool:
    Two 13" x 15" Louisiana Hot Sauce #2266 HB
    Two 2" x 14½" Collards #1277
    Two 2" x 12" Collards #1277
    Mustard #1224 for the stocking
    Parchment #1110 for the cuff
    Louisiana Hot Sauce #2266 for the stripes and berries
    Collards #1277 for the Heel, toe, and holly
Green thread
Poly-Fil stuffing

INSTRUCTIONS:

CUTTING:
    Two 13" x 15" Louisiana Hot Sauce HB wool.
    Two 2" x 14½" pieces from Collards wool.
    Two 2" x 12" pieces from Collards wool.
    Large stocking from Gold wool.
    Pattern pieces #1, 2, and 3 from Red wool.
    Holly, heel, and toe from Green wool.
    Cuff from Parchment wool.
    Berry from Red wool.

ASSEMBLY:

1. Lay a 2" x 12" strip across top and bottom edges of one of the 13" x 15" rectangles.
2. Pin the outer edge of the Green strips about ¼" from the outer edge of the Red rectangle.
3. Lay a 2" x 14½" strip on each side of rectangle, lining up the edges ¼" from the edge.
4. Buttonhole stitch the strips to the rectangle to hold them in place.
5. Lay the Gold stocking down on the center. Lay the Red stripes on top.
6. Add the heel and the toe. Position the cuff on top.
7. Put holly and berry on top of cuff. Pin pieces in place.
8. Buttonhole stitch or Whipstitch around stocking pieces using Green thread.
9. Lay the two 13" x 15" Red rectangles right sides together.
10. Stitch around edges using a ¼" seam, leaving 6" opening for turning.
11. Turn right side out. Push out corners.
12. Stuff firmly with Poly-Fil. Hand stitch opening closed.

Stockings

photo on page 15

1

See
Stocking
pattern
on
page 43.

2

3

Holly

Berry

heel

toe

cuff

Stockings

photo on page 15

Framed Stocking

Punch Needle
- see page 17

SIZE:
  Punch needle 2½" x 4½"

MATERIALS:
Weeks Dye Works #5 pearl cotton:
  Turkish Red #2266
  Holly #1279
  Gold #2221
  Whitewash #1091
8" square Weaver's cloth
5" x 7" frame

INSTRUCTIONS:
1. Punch Red berries.
2. Punch Green holly.
3. Punch heel and toe with Holly color.
4. Punch Gold sections of stocking.
5. Punch Red sections of stocking.
6. Outline and fill in the cuff with Whitewash.
7. See page 17 for finishing instructions.

Snowman Mug Rug

Punch Needle - see page 17

SIZE: 3½" x 4"

MATERIALS:
Weeks Dye Works #5 pearl cotton:
  2 Charcoal #1303
  Turkish Red #2226
  Noel #4105 for letters and hat
  Snowflakes #4125
DMC #5 pearl cotton Orange #947
7" square Weaver's cloth
3¾" x 4" felt or wool to finish the back

INSTRUCTIONS:
1. Punch the letters S-N-O-W and the hat using Noel color.
2. Punch the carrot nose using Orange.
3. Punch the eyes using Charcoal color.
4. Punch the scarf and top of hat using Turkish Red.
5. Punch the snowman body using Snowflakes.
6. Outline and fill in the background using Charcoal.
7. See page 17 for finishing instructions.

Snowman and Holly

photo on page 16

Framed Gingerbread
Punch Needle - see page 17

SIZE:
    Punch needle 4" x 5"

MATERIALS:
Weeks Dye Works #5 pearl cotton:
    Chestnut #1269
    Hazelnut #2237
    Fawn #1111
DMC #5 pearl cotton
    (Red #115, Black #310 for eyes)
8" square Weaver's cloth
8" x 10" frame

INSTRUCTIONS:
1. Punch Red in bowl and hearts using Red.
2. Punch center gingerbread man using Chestnut.
3. Punch remaining 2 Gingerbread men using Hazelnut.
4. Punch bowl using Fawn.
5. Using Black, make French Knots for gingerbread men eyes.
6. See page 17 for finishing instructions.

Gingerbread Men

photo on page 16

right
gingerbread

2

1

1

2

3

O

left
gingerbread

Bowl

center
gingerbread

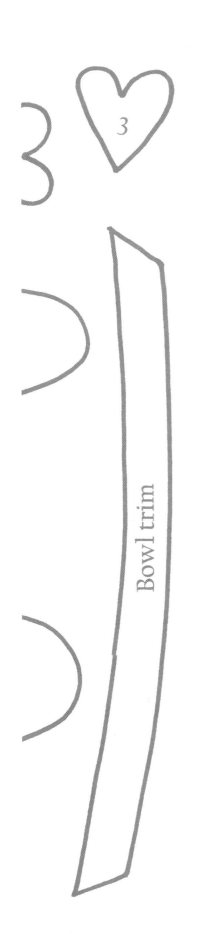

Bowl trim

Placement for Pillow

Gingerbread Pillow
Wool Work - see page 18

SIZE: 12" x 15"

MATERIALS:

Weeks Dye Works Wool:
> One 10" x 13" hand-dyed Deep Red for inner background fabric
> Two 12" x 15" Chestnut #1269 for outer background
> Sand #3500 for bowl
> Deep Sea #2104 for bowl trim
> Meadow #2176 for leaves
> Chestnut #1269 for center gingerbread
> Palomino #1232 for left and right gingerbread

DMC #5 pearl cotton Charcoal #3021 for eyes

Brown thread

Poly-Fil stuffing

INSTRUCTIONS:

1. Cut out all pieces and assemble on the Red wool background.
2. Using Brown pearl cotton, make French knots for the eyes of all of the gingerbread men.
3. Using the Brown thread, Buttonhole stitch around each piece to affix to background.
4. Center the Red wool piece on top of Brown wool background piece.
5. Buttonhole stitch around the edges of the Red wool piece to affix it to the Brown wool background.
6. Lay the 12" x 15" rectangles right sides together.
7. Stitch around edge using ¼" seam, leaving 6" opening for turning.
8. Turn right sides out. Push out corners.
9. Stuff firmly with Poly-Fil. Hand stitch opening closed.

Pansies

photo on page 11

SUPPLIERS -

Most craft and variety stores carry an excellent assortment of supplies. If you need something special, ask your local store to contact the following companies:

PUNCH NEEDLE
EMBROIDERY PROJECTS
  www.prairiegrovepeddler.com
CAMEO PUNCH NEEDLES
  www.punchneedlemarketplace.com
CTR NEEDLES
  www.ctrneedleworks.com
IGOLOCHKOY RUSSIAN PUNCH NEEDLES
  www.gailbird.com.com
SUPPLIES
  Norden Crafts, www.nordencrafts.com
PEARL COTTON AND HAND DYED WOOL
  Weeks Dye Works, 877-683-7393, Garner, NC
  DMC, 973-589-0606, S. Kearny, NJ

MANY THANKS to my friends for their cheerful help and wonderful ideas!
Kathy McMillan • Jennifer Laughlin
Janet Long • Janie Ray • Donna Kinsey
David & Donna Thomason

Many thanks to Beth Davis for all her help.

Framed Purple Pansies

Punch Needle - see page 17

SIZE:
  Punch Needle 3¾" x 4"

MATERIALS:
Weeks Dye Works #5 pearl cotton:
  Saffron #2223
  Whitewash #109
  Emerald #2171
  Iris #2316
DMC #5 pearl cotton Dark Purple #550
8" square Weaver's cloth
5" x 7" frame

INSTRUCTIONS:
1. Punch lines on upper center of each flower in Whitewash.
2. Punch lines on lower center of each flower in Saffron.
3. Punch area around that in Dark Purple.
4. Fill in each flower with Iris.
5. Punch leaves & stems with Emerald.
6. Background was not filled in, but may be filled in if desired.
7. See page 17 for finishing instructions.

Framed Painted Daisies

Punch Needle - see page 17

SIZE:
  Punch Needle 3¾" x 4"

MATERIALS:
Weeks Dye Works #5 pearl cotton: 2 Camellia #2276
  DMC #5 pearl cotton Green #471, Gold #742
7" square Weavers cloth
5" x 7" frame

INSTRUCTIONS:
1. Punch flower centers with Gold.
2. Punch flowers with Camellia.
3. Punch leaves and stems with Green.
4. Background was not filled in, but may be filled in if desired.
5. See page 17 for finishing instructions.